Do Not

Cow Sprouts

INTRO TO PHASE 5

/ou/

Level 4+
Blue+

Helpful Hints for Reading at Home

The graphemes (written letters) and phonemes (units of sound) used throughout this series are aligned with Letters and Sounds. This offers a consistent approach to learning whether reading at home or in the classroom.

THIS BLUE+ BOOK BAND SERVES AS AN INTRODUCTION TO PHASE 5. EACH BOOK IN THIS BAND USES ALL PHONEMES LEARNED UP TO PHASE 4, WHILE INTRODUCING ONE PHASE 5 PHONEME. HERE IS A LIST OF PHONEMES FOR THIS PHASE, WITH THE NEW PHASE 5 PHONEME. AN EXAMPLE OF THE PRONUNCIATION CAN BE FOUND IN BRACKETS.

Phase 3			
j (jug)	v (van)	w (wet)	x (fox)
y (yellow)	z (zoo)	zz (buzz)	qu (quick)
ch (chip)	sh (shop)	th (thin/then)	ng (ring)
ai (rain)	ee (feet)	igh (night)	oa (boat)
oo (boot/look)	ar (farm)	or (for)	ur (hurt)
ow (cow)	oi (coin)	ear (dear)	air (fair)
ure (sure)	er (corner)		

New Phase 5 Phoneme	ou (foul, sprouts, sound)

HERE ARE SOME WORDS WHICH YOUR CHILD MAY FIND TRICKY.

Phase 4 Tricky Words			
said	were	have	there
like	little	so	one
do	when	some	out
come	what		

TOP TIPS FOR HELPING YOUR CHILD TO READ:

- Allow children time to break down unfamiliar words into units of sound and then encourage children to string these sounds together to create the word.
- Encourage your child to point out any focus phonics when they are used.
- Read through the book more than once to grow confidence.
- Ask simple questions about the text to assess understanding.
- Encourage children to use illustrations as prompts.

INTRO TO PHASE 5

/ou/

This book introduces the phoneme /ou/ and is a Blue+ Level 4+ book band.

Do Not Feed the Cow Sprouts

Written by
Robin Twiddy

Illustrated by
Emre Karacan

"Do not feed the cow sprouts," Dan shouts. But the cow had been fed.

So, Dan jumps up and out of his bed.

There is a loud trumping sound from the cow's rear.

Dan thinks that it is the loudest sound he ever did hear.

The room fills with a foul smell. Dan runs out. He is not feeling well.

The next room smells sweet, but not for long. Soon there is a cloud of cow pong.

Dan runs to get out. Can Dan outrun the smell?

No, he cannot. Dan trips on a rug and is sad that he fell.

Get up, Dan, and get a peg. This might help, Dan thinks.

Ouch, the pinch of the peg is too strong.
Dan blinks.

Pegs do not help. Pegs just hurt! Get out, Dan. Quick!

Dan can see a hound. The hound can sniff the smell but then the hound feels sick.

The shack is filling with the smell. Dan needs to get out!

But he cannot get out. There is a lock!
Dan begins to shout.

"Help, help! They fed the cow sprouts, and I cannot get out!"

"We must not feed the cow the sprouts," Dan shouts.

Dan runs up to get out of the stink.

He runs up and up. Dan needs to think.

He cannot keep running up. He is running out of stairs!

Can he block the smell with a pair of trousers? But how will he get a pair?

No, it will not do. The smell is in the attic and it is all Dan can think about.

Dan cannot go up. He must smash. This brick will get him out!

A toss and the brick hits. Smash!
The smell is at his back, so Dan must be quick.

If he jumps in the pond he will not be hurt. Dan feels sick.

Splash! The smell is out and Dan is out!

Do not ever, ever, ever feed a cow sprouts!

Do Not Feed the Cow Sprouts

1) Where is Dan at the beginning of the story?

2) What does Dan put on his nose to stop the smell?

3) How do you think Dan felt when he got to the top of the shack?

4) What does Dan use to smash his way out of the shack?

a) A brick

b) Sprouts

c) A peg

5) What does Dan jump into?

BookLife PUBLISHING

BookLife Readers

King's Lynn, Norfolk PE30 4LS

ISBN 978-1-80155-055-0

A catalogue record for this book is available from the British Library.

Do Not Feed the Cow Sprouts
Written by Robin Twiddy
Illustrated by Emre Karacan

An Introduction to BookLife Readers...

Our Readers have been specifically created in line with the London Institute of Education's approach to book banding and are phonetically decodable and ordered to support each phase of the Letters and Sounds document.

Each book has been created to provide the best possible reading and learning experience. Our aim is to share our love of books with children, providing both emerging readers and prolific page-turners with beautiful books that are guaranteed to provoke interest and learning, regardless of ability.

BOOK BAND GRADED using the Institute of Education's approach to levelling.

PHONETICALLY DECODABLE supporting each phase of Letters and Sounds.

EXERCISES AND QUESTIONS to offer reinforcement and to ascertain comprehension.

BEAUTIFULLY ILLUSTRATED to inspire and provoke engagement, providing a variety of styles for the reader to enjoy whilst reading through the series.

AUTHOR INSIGHT:
ROBIN TWIDDY

Robin Twiddy is one of BookLife Publishing's most creative and prolific editorial talents, who imbues all his copy with a sense of adventure and energy. Robin's Cambridge-based first class honours degree in psychosocial studies offers a unique viewpoint on factual information and allows him to relay information in a manner that readers of any age are guaranteed to retain. He also holds a certificate in Teaching in the Lifelong Sector, and a postgraduate certificate in Consumer Psychology.

A father of two, Robin has written over 70 titles for BookLife and specialises in conceptual, role-playing narratives which promote interaction with the reader and inspire even the most reluctant of readers to fully engage with his books.

INTRO TO PHASE 5
/ou/

This book introduces the phoneme /ou/ and is a Blue+ Level 4+ book band.